An Incremental Life

Poems

Luci Shaw

PARACLETE PRESS
BREWSTER, MASSACHUSETTS

2025 First Printing

An Incremental Life: Poems

ISBN 978-1-64060-979-2

Library of Congress Cataloging-in-Publication Data
Names: Shaw, Luci, author.
Title: An incremental life : poems / Luci Shaw.
Description: Brewster, Massachusetts : Paraclete Press, 2025. | Series: Iron pen | Summary: "In these poems, Shaw breathes life into the simpleness of the every-day and finds God in the memory of the mundane"— Provided by publisher.
Identifiers: LCCN 2024051571 (print) | LCCN 2024051572 (ebook) | ISBN 9781640609792 (trade paperback) | ISBN 9781640609808 (epub)
Subjects: LCGFT: Religious poetry.
Classification: LCC PS3569.H384 I53 2025 (print) | LCC PS3569.H384 (ebook) | DDC 811/.54--dc23/eng/20241106
LC record available at https://lccn.loc.gov/2024051571
LC ebook record available at https://lccn.loc.gov/2024051572
10 9 8 7 6 5 4 3 2 1

Published by Paraclete Press
Brewster, Massachusetts
www.paracletepress.com

Printed in the United States of America

Praise for An Incremental life

"There's so much to ponder, appreciate, and learn from Luci Shaw's words. And so, once more, in this, her latest volume of poems, *An Incremental Life*. What especially strikes me in reading her this time around is how she manages to blend the music of poetry with what prayer can sound like, here in our dailiness—in the whisper of trees, the flight of birds, in preparing a meal and breaking bread for others, as well as in those recollections of youth and of those here now only in memory and the radiance of naming them, and then in meditating on our own mortality as the years go by. All of it made fuller by evoking the blessings—in light and in darkness—there for the taking, if we but took the time, like Luci Shaw, to see what is there before us."

—**Paul Mariani,** author of *Deaths and Transfigurations*, *The Mystery of It All*, and *All That Will be New*

"Luci Shaw's latest collection, *An Incremental Life*, sings of the bright intervals in a cherished soul whose life's oeuvre hums with a perpetual, hopeful delight for our weary sojourners. In her ninth decade, Shaw's flourishing world of flora and fauna continues to bear fruit and multiply in the garden of her richly allusive, metaphorical imagination. Here is a wellspring of musical wisdom and meaningful sustenance where the 'Faithful One' plays 'the ear of / my mind like an instrument,' blessing life's very small yet vital increments of lived experience, tender and tenacious moments ethereal yet embodied as 'single / breaths of an ambient air.'"

—**Karen An-hwei Lee**, author of *The Beautiful Immunity* and *Duress*

"For decades I have sat at Luci Shaw's feet, listening to her lyrical wisdom, her playful music, her spiritual insight, and her deep connectedness to the natural world. In *An Incremental Life*, Luci Shaw shares her metapoetics choosing 'words like matches, / striking them to see what happens next.' As a nonagenarian, she acknowledges her shrinking life, yet invites us even into this experience. Still she wrestles with faith, and says to God, 'Come, now. Fill / the gaps, mend the widening cracks in my aging /soul. I'm moving in your direction, but I move / more slowly, see more dimly, require more daily.' As always, though, Luci Shaw is as wide-eyed as a child. 'My heart,' she writes, 'is ambushed by simple beauty.'"

—**D. S. Martin**, Poet-in-Residence, McMaster Divinity College, and author of *Angelicus*

Also by Luci Shaw

POETRY

Listen to the Green
The Secret Trees
Postcard from the Shore
Polishing the Petoskey Stone
Writing the River
The Angles of Light
The Green Earth
Waterlines
What the Light Was Like
Harvesting Fog
Scape
Eye of the Beholder
The Generosity
Angels Everywhere
Reversing Entropy

FOR CHILDREN

The Genesis of It all
The O in Hope

WITH MADELEINE L'ENGLE

Winter Song
A Prayerbook for Spiritual Friends
Friends for the Journey

NONFICTION

God in the Dark
Life Path
Water My Soul
The Crime of Living Cautiously
Breath for the Bones
Adventure of Ascent
The Thumbprint in the Clay

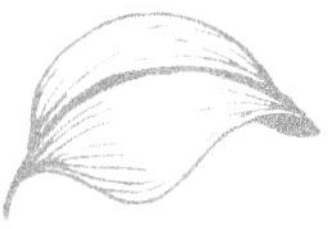

As always, Karen Cooper has my deep gratitude for her help, over many months, in shaping these poems for publication.

INTRODUCTION

Amaryllis!

During the days of abbreviated daylight in later November and early December, and in the weeks leading up to Christmas, I feel the deep need to push back against the realities of winter darkness and chill.

One of the deficits I feel most deeply at this time of year is the way our garden's growth has slowed, finally shutting down and going dormant for the winter. The slowing and gloom of those darker days is a kind of deficit that affects me emotionally and spiritually, as well as physically. I can almost balance it out by reminding myself that, though my soul is deprived of lush garden growth and splendid displays of color, winter is a season for a different scale of value.

I'm grateful for the activity in this phase of living that moves ahead in slower, more relaxed, often more gratifying increments. An incremental life is one of small gains, or victories, of growth achieved gradually, of actions occurring one at a time, in a more measured sequence than what is experienced earlier, when energy and motivation are at their peak.

One practical solution for the lack of a joyfully blooming garden in winter is to bring the garden inside. In our house, with its warmth and comfort, I find great satisfaction in creating a kind of inside garden. The large, west-facing windows in our kitchen and dining room give us access to the wide and restless beauty of Bellingham Bay and the islands of Puget Sound. In the light those windows provide I can watch my potted plants grow, their leaves greening and blooms gleaming as they flourish and decorate our interior living.

An inside plant is a joy to tend and observe the slow and deliberate changes in its vegetable life span. Sometimes, in my own wintering body, I am profoundly aware of the need to sit back and slow down in the pace of my living.

So, in November, I order half a dozen amaryllis bulbs, each of them holding a bright promise: a chance for us to enjoy some of the many varied combinations of vivid growth and color.

The amaryllis bulbs come packed individually in their pots, covered with a fibrous mulch, mangy-looking and decidedly unattractive, with their peeling, scaly husks. But I have faith, trusting in the miraculous changes brought about by life and light. I believe that as I plant each of the bulbs in a pot of soil and water it, it will reward us, growing in the light and filling the room with brilliant amaryllis color. So I brush away the mulch and expose the top of each bulb, then place the pots in a row along our kitchen windowsill. I bring a couple of the potted bulbs into my office, where they sit on a window ledge above my desk, absorbing light and warmth. Then, I wait.

In winter, the time seems to pass slowly, in minor increments. But as I wait my days are full of good things—reading, writing, praying, waiting, hoping, nourishing the friendships that bring emotional and spiritual color into my life.

You cannot force growth for amaryllis bulbs, and with these babies a wait is imperative: a week, or three, until, in one of the pots, a small green tongue pokes up from the bulb's ugly, scaly surface. It feels hopeful, like a baby being born.

As the days pass and more green, strap-like leaves rise from the bulbs in their pots, I watch for the next stage—a swelling, a fattening at the tip of a stem, where a bloom is ripening under a pointed green cap. This expectation demands a life of faith, the way praying opens up a view of the Creator God, who is constantly at work in enlarging our lives. *Incremental*—the word takes on fresh meaning in the context of the slow growth of plants.

Hidden within their coats of green, my amaryllises are growing into full maturity. Though their development and flowering are still incremental, here and there I'm seeing the swellings that protrude, fleshing out and elongating into buds at the tips of the tall green stems.

One winter morning I'm greeted by the flaming, flaunting red burst of a flower that I have been waiting for. It is like a bell ringing, and glorious, well worth the wait!

My desk calendar reminds me of all the days it has taken and the patience that was needed to accomplish the flowering of those dry, dark, hairy bulbs. My long, full, human life, with multiple opportunities for creative growth and activity, rewards me with the possibility of reaching true maturity and wholeness. As I live into my late 90s I long, still, for an overflowing state of mind, body, and spirit in which the Creator God may find satisfaction.

I can live only one day at a time, and my hope is to live that one day fully and richly, showing the minor increments of growth and maturity that attest to God's divine purpose and patience in my life.

—*Luci Shaw*

Contents

Testaments

Sacraments

Increments

I live by increments, single
breaths of an ambient air,
marking off hours, days.

Apprenticed to grace, I tread *statio*
in sequentiae, edging every step
forward before venturing the next.

Staggering up towards the stony
crests of the foothills, dusty, I am
almost undone with weariness, only half
believing that the view will widen.

In my falling upward into your home,
O Faithful One, stay with me,
your wind music playing the ear of
my mind like an instrument.

Increments

Nutriment

Reading a poem aloud along with your eggs
and coffee is like adding good bread—
your mouth loving the ordinary, whole-grain words
spilling over the poem's lip. You drink in the sounds
of language like musical notes.

Swirl them with the voice in your brain. Relish
the syllables; taste them with your insatiable tongue.
Words will leap from the lines in stanzas.
Slipping, agile, mental images will dissolve
within you, become your diet.

Bleed

Raggedly, the knife bites into my
fingertip, the blood springing instantly
out of the cut curve of flesh, overflowing
the raw edges of skin.

I lift my hand to heaven. The blood
slows, oozes past knuckle, down
wrist and arm, unstoppable. A scarlet drop
falls to the white-tiled bathroom floor.

The small planet, like all fluids, echoes
the form of Earth, drops of oil that float
on water, rain, tears, hail, the pupil in
every eye, the configuration gleaming red

from the tile below.

"Newborns"

Like seeds from an exotic fruit, their tiny heads
beam up at us, the bald pink of the newly born.
Twins—the double offspring of their teenage
Karen mother—on the X-rays their matchstick
skeletons show white against black. I view them
online, for survival, from a far distance, their world
under threat from bombs, warfare, poverty and disease.
Thanks to technology, but thanks more fervently
to skillful human love and care, we have become
acquainted. Though they rest on the small screen
of my cell phone deep in the pocket of my jeans,
I hold them deeper, in the heart sac of my prayers.

I Remember My Father

John Northcote Deck

When I think of my father
here's what I remember—
how the rough warmth
of his tweed jacket felt
when he hugged me, or bent down
to kiss the top of my head, me,
playing Bach on the piano—
a difficult fugue that he loved,
though I never mastered it.

Also his masculine smell,
how it comes back to me
with that music.

His craggy face showed up
on my computer screen
the other day. It felt like
an intentional message.
I welcomed it, hoping for it
to happen again.

I hold close the vivid clues
of my life at ten years of age,

at twelve, his challenge to me and my
little brother: to swim the lake,
a mile across, and we did it.

It's my father who shows up
most vividly in memory, I, his first child,
born when he was sixty, remember
how he scorned lettuce and salads,
"rabbit food" he'd mutter.

Just yesterday I polished
the silver ring that clasped
his folded linen napkin on the family
dinner table, engraved ND.

Even now, certain angles
of sunlight across our rose-colored
living room carpet remind me
of the time he and I brought home
the pink rug from Turkey
we'd bought for my mother's
birthday.

How completely he loved God—
he could sit in the corner of
a crowded room, face lifted,

beaming, utterly enjoying
a heavenly presence of which
the others were unaware.

A book of poems
bears his inscription on
the flyleaf, given when I
went off to college.
"To my darling daughter,
With much love, Daddy."

To read almost any poem,
is like a key turning, opening
a door for him to come in.

Brain in a Jar

My neuropathologist brother,
accustomed to examining nerve tissue,
obtained and kept, in a jar on his office
shelf, the brain of Glenn Gould.
Recorded performances of the celebrated
Canadian pianist stirred John's
awed delight. Gould's frequent habit
was to hum along as he played.
My brother, a lover of the eccentric,
found this habit beguiling. For years,
the specimen gleamed behind glass,
its pale, convoluted tissue a phantom
presence for John and his visitors.

My brother and his office are long gone,
along with the bottle and its resident.
Do those old visitors remember the
spectral presence in its jar, attended by
a gentle, ghostly hum?

The Pages of the Mind

The ink in the barrel of the pen in my hand
swirls darkly with words not even brought
to mind. Yet. My journal's blank pages lie open,
waiting, like me, to watch what happens, when
it happens. It all depends. Plans for the week,
the month, the year may well dissolve the way
multiple drops of rain fall and are lost in
the Pacific. The brain may yield an unexpected
emerald tide of memories—ferns deep in
the rain forest, the pale geographics on sycamore
bark, the rainbow gleams from fish scales before
the fish dies, and dulls. Shapes and colors glint
and scurry. A single feather that puts a wing
in mind. The sharp sight of blood from a cut
finger. All this before night's oblivion carries away
the day's gains, its losses, its possibilities.

Donation: Hand-Knit Cardigan

Here, take it, it is all I have to offer,
though it is unfinished, unfinishing,
doubtful that it will ever be finished.
My fingers clumsy with age and arthritis,
the knitted seams wait for joining, as if
the unfinished sleeve is its own end-of-
life destiny, its evidence of mortality's
scourge. As old memory's loosening skein
attempts to mend it, to sew the seams,
to pull together what remains of an old
skill, though the knitting itself remains
uneven, ragged, seams unsewn, yarn
faded, coffee-stained, the garment gaping
through its own sagging armholes.
A reject, though from behind the fabric
a scrape of light shines through, still.
Yes, Thank you. Thank you. That is all.

The Imperatives of Speech

Getting older means sensing senescence
taking over, its dark hand grasping, fingers
not letting go. Along with language, easy
movement, sound sleep, some of the joys
in living drain away. I suck in the arduous air
with effort, a vexing and anxious wind
in the door. This, and a stiffness of the bones
means I must apologize, staggering to
the nearest chair, "Wait, don't gossip or tell
good jokes until I'm sitting down. I need
to breathe before I laugh." My voice is
gravelly as loose stones under the feet.
I cough, trying for a clear tone, and cough
again, and only then, and haltingly, can I
join in conversation, before the flow
of ideas congeals, before I lose track, fail
to respond, my nimble commentary lost.

Map

A road is a poem writing
its long lyric across a landscape.

Rising, falling, well-traveled
or solitary—a unique signature

on the land. In unknown
territory, I may need to follow

a map. What I am learning
is that an intersection offers

a new perspective. As pilgrim,
I let myself be challenged

by a steeply winding future,
watching for signs of adventure,

around the bend, or just over
the next hill. . . .

Foiled

This day of the week, this beautiful
day of play planned for Pebble Beach,
with breakers unfurling themselves
across pale reaches of sand—why is this the day
my shoulder, that stalwart joint in an
architecture of bones, fails me, suddenly
shot through with shafts of anguish. But perhaps,
a quick swallow of a pain pill that carries in its
small purse a temporary relief . . .

So now I lie on the afternoon bed, waiting,
like a sinner after confession, for forgiveness,
for mercy to present itself. Perhaps time,
then, for a swim, or at least a stay of execution,
the pain sent out on parole. Now the ocean,
in its beautiful energy, its great, foaming waves
gathering, gathering, waits for my healing
to be realized, my freedom for play to become
available, achievable, until the ocean's
deep reservoir of urgency is released,
in an inevitability of thunder.

Grand Canyon

Casual sightseers for a day in the desert,
we revisit the continent's mighty yawn,
a cavernous, open mouth, purple-hazed
in late afternoon. Driving easily, close to
the canyon rim, we stop the car often, to stare,
speaking our amazement, as if assuring
each other of its reality. Deep down, below,
a thready current carves a way south, gravid,
pebbled. We recall how, twenty years ago,
the same flow's fierce turbulence
had carried our raft downstream, tossing us
like toys in the fluent current as we,
intoxicated by adventure, gazed up, up
the walls of rock shaped steeply by time,
and the rough, sculpting hands of water.

Then, late this afternoon, an astonishment;
far below the canyon rim a small, barely
surviving trickle gleams, victim of our national
drought. To our shame, our sorrow,
our consumer generation has drained the river's
fluid rush, diverting it for our own perverse,
self-serving use. Yet even now, in the deep canyon,
with its sparse, sandy edges, water persists,

though barely, its trickle overgrown with tamarisk,
seepwillow, spiny camel-thorn, cotton-weed,
brittlebush, and arrow-weed, so that where,
in springtime, floods would have washed away
all growth, all greenery, today the water-flow,
heated in the sun, evaporates, spits, pools,
shrunken, its generous flow barely remembered.
Endangered, a crouching animal, the flow
struggles, evidence of our negligence,
our lack of vision, our national disgrace.

"Vertigo"

Every day now, January's sun opens its eye
a few seconds earlier, marking one day less in
my life's small span. Yet it is my desire, still,

to fulfill whatever beauty is my calling.
I knit and knit, making the same mistake
over and over. Or stand, shaking, at the center

of a revolving world, staggering across the kitchen
to water the plants on the windowsill, trembling
for the fear of falling. Hanging onto

the handrails of aging, I stumble through a day,
incapable, even, of crossing the road to
the mailbox. And the wind, the wind, the chill

wind—how it buffets our house, singing
its bitter song, trapped in the window with
a choked sound like a wail, a sob.

Surprise

Spring is always an astonishment. You'd think
by now we'd know what to expect, be ready
and waiting, after all our decades of year in, year out.
Yet we're surprised that it's so surprising,
so welcome, so soul-gladdening, this God-gift of
a waking, warming, dandelion season.

It's as if we've forgotten, or have taken for granted
the how and why of Eastertide, when, like our
fasting souls, the dry sticks and stalks of winter
begin again to flesh out, succulent, freshly green
from drinking in a silver rain—such a heaven gift!
The amazement! As we're once again jubilant
at the arousal, the flush and flash of wind gusts
hitting the windows with a succession of wet kisses.
We welcome this strong weather, this God-gift
that knocks off the scabs of our chill winter,
leaving us new, new, greenly eager to give praise for
heavenly mercies, as announced in the daily forecast.

Now, let us be noisily glad and give thanks. Again!
Again! Let us never tire of giving God our verdant
expectations and our jubilant gratitudes.

Estuary

October, the nights are turning crystal clear.
Evening, and we drive down to the waterfront
to investigate what was announced in our
morning paper—the formation of a new estuary
that cuts a fresh channel between an old, freshwater
stream and the salty tides of Bellingham Bay.

The news, fresh and intriguing enough for us
to want to investigate, drives us shoreward.
Above us a sickle moon's up-tilted crescent seems
to pour, as from a glowing bowl, a fresh flow of light.

We look at each other, a wordless glance
of agreement that says—*Here we are, together*
experiencing this magical evening, our old eyes
viewing a celestial transaction as if for the first time.
And, as the tides pour in and out, again, again,
our two joined lives create and acknowledge their own
intimate exchange, our very human intertidal flow.

Methow Valley Landscape

The contoured hills with their huge, naked shoulders
loom above the valley, overlooking the gleaming Methow
running south. In the fertile valley, farmland sprinklers
spread their green circles, and the herds of cattle
shift slowly, browsing across the pastures, their bovine
bodies dark against the painterly emerald fields.
Above, clouds flow and break with deliberate speed,
shadowing the landscape like moving camouflage,
transient always, their beauty unreliable. May I be
saved from that cloud-vagueness. May I practice
the stance of the ancient hills, putting on fresh light daily.

Mosquito Lake Road

November, 2023

Driving Mosquito Lake Road, a long forest loop,
keeps doubling back on itself as if admitting
a mistake and trying again. And again.

And Mosquito Lake is not really a lake, more like an
embroidered bog. Today, everything is golden—
the day and hour destined for the big-leaf maples

to undress themselves. Out for a drive, and now
we are simply parked, watching. No breath of wind,
no haste, but this is the exact time for each tree

to unstitch its bruised yellow leaves, one, then
another, and one more, and so on, each floating
down the still air to rest on the muddy track.

As if this is nightfall, time for everything to
settle in for the long winter sleep, time for God to
snuff out the last lights of the known world.

Elements

Just Add Water

(with apologies to Richard Powers)

The world is greening. The mosses'
slow, unstoppable surge across rocks
consoles the eye with soft.

The maple leaves open wide
their five-fingered hands to welcome
the sun's bright overtures.

Even on a still day, aspens
shake their leaves
in an invisible wind.

We've watched the forests,
attentive over a smattering of seasons, grow
at the speed of wood.

Their branches of knowledge subsist with
a charming shyness that belies
their unstoppable force.

Slow, certain, the faerie systems
are being birthed from earth into air,
while some communities of plants, willful
and crafty, plan to take over the world.

Garden Work

Look at a garden, almost any garden, and it will
look back at you, breathing an essential loveliness
in your direction. It will not stop work in the evening

but all night long the world's beauty will seep into
the soil, the air. Into you, too, as you engage in
a conversation with the Seed Sower. Acknowledge

and respond to the loving care, the diligent digging,
the forming of furrows, the patient sowing of seeds,
the covering, then, with damp soil. The waiting

for the holy breath of Weather to speak loving-kindness
and tender mercy into the sprouts that shoot up
into the wideness of air. Then pause, considering

the yield of hand work, the heart work. Smell
the fragrant air. Lay aside, for a few moments, the world's
struggles. Let the blessing of the garden enter you.

Over and Under

for Richard Powers

Written movingly, and with a verdant artistry,
botanists tell the overstory story, about the
magic realm where green and growth reach up
from dark and dim to vivid and wide and sky.
Others study the understory, what rots from
lack of light, the decayed, in turn, turning a dark,
secret bedding of humus that nurtures shy
root and seed, promise and disclosure, a thriving
network for survival. Resisting devastation as
exemplar for human communities—friends
carrying the messages of hopeful flourishing into
dark suffering and struggle. Respect what lives
quietly beneath, above, within, around. Protect it,
serving it, thriving within it, never ignoring it,
or losing it, and all its dark richness.

Clematis Integrifolia

Planted, already, on our
roadside trellis, her petals,
according to the label,
integrated—those tiny,
startling blue flowers
join in our admiration
of their own loveliness.

Perhaps it's another word
for false modesty as they
hang their tiny indigo bells
face down from their lattice,
hoping for the esteem
of visitors and passers-by.

Quanta

October 4, 2023

Major announcement in today's news:
three research scientists, one of them
a woman, who, years ago had drilled down
into reality and identified *nano* particles,

bits of reality so small they call them
quantum dots. Now, finally, their research
has been recognized as significant enough
to win the Nobel Prize in Chemistry.

The "dots," particles, infinitely small
packages of reality, once considered insignificant,
even negligent, are now recognized as achieving
primal value in the making of meaning.

Like God's most insignificant creatures,
each particle is understood to be packed tight
with electrons, with an energy powerful
enough to effect the making and sustaining

of the universe. Negligent? We might call this
one of God's mightiest Creative works.

Ambush of the Heart

You, primal Artist, irresistible!
Your glory is etched on my soul!

My heart is ambushed by simple beauty.
Bird song. Sunlight on corn stubble.

And today, as I watched a froth of white
bubbling along the horizon,

I was helplessly happy, vulnerable to
the simplicity of light shining on clouds.

Sometimes I unearth a memory
like a precious stone, a gold ring,

I welcome it without reservation,
writing it down to capture it,

allowing myself a creative lacuna
in which to contemplate it, this delight

for the soul, wondering
how everything adds up to unreasonable

happiness. Say you've discovered
a folded diagram in the map drawer.

You suddenly remember—that guy
hiking the Sierra! You'd shared

a drink before moving on. Or the detailed
map of a coastal highway

that once stretched, charmingly, before us
as we drove—sandy beaches between headlands,

a lagoon, or two—simple enchantment.
See? The arousal of re-discovery,
as we discern God breathing life into

our storied memories, connecting
the scattered events of our beautiful life.

Flawed

I sing my human imperfection—
cat not yet fed, the bed half-made.
On a hot day the shift of shade
moved from where I'd planned to rest.
The mounting sum of bills unpaid.
The wall clock stopped at half-past time.
Unfinished tasks, sin unconfessed.
An earring lost, an awkward rhyme.
A poem begun, but incomplete.
A painful sore that needs to heal.
Leftovers from a family meal.
Dishes unwashed. My muddy feet
from morning's walk. I'm running late.
Confession that is mere pretense.
All the unfinished tasks that wait.
Prevenient grace I long to know.
God hear me now, I pray to sense
your loving blessings' generous flow.

Glimpsed

The country road, after a heavy rain,
has become a shining river, like an ascent
to heaven. I am graced by the gasps of light,
a holy brightness rising from the nearby
field of oats, so lavishly green, with their
seed heads' soft promises toward
a breakfast cereal, to be consumed with milk,
a hint of brown sugar, and a prayer.

Refresh

From the sun-ghosted grass, roadside,
the voices of light speak a morning's
awakening. Listen, and look up, until the sun
itself refreshes you with gleam and glisten.
Now, bare your soul of everything but this
heart-lifting moment. Then, as you keep
walking, you may come to a fast-flowing
stream in which you recognize an image
of the holy.

You take off your shoes and,
barefoot and up to your knees, you step
into the force-flow of its chill, until your flesh
is numb, but your spirit tingles. Acknowledge it;
you are living a metaphor. Your body
images forth your spirit's longing for
an immersive blessing, for the piercing
presence of your holy God.

Nest:

the hatchling speaks

As soon as I
cracked the shell
I knew I had to fly

so little time to ponder
the requirements
of aviation

or enjoy the warm refuge
of nest, and a steady supply
of comestibles

perhaps insects
with a beakful of
crunchy
wings

but not yet, not
now, before I get
certified

Oh, if only
I could wait
for a complement of
feathers

or train with
some expert whose
history in

air miles
set world records. But not
now. Not ready or
not willing
to risk it, though
the wide air beckons,
and it's
time . . .

Birds

Along the freeway, heading south, glimpsed, the sudden,
ordinary glory of iridescence. A pigeon's wings

opening and closing, landing on an overpass railing.

Later, for an afternoon's rest and reading, we park,
half-hidden,
at the bushy end of a wetlands path.

Like the pigeon, we have found a place to settle,
to park our car, to relax our bodies, to free our minds.

By a rusty faucet we see a faded notice that forbids its use for
a car wash. We shake our heads. We have no such intention.

Our plan: to read. To absorb the afternoon's light,
its quiet calm. To wait and see what happens . . . If anything
happens.

From our sheltered corner we overlook a wideness of mudflats,
the creep of an incoming tide,

Which matches our mood comfortably.

Behind us, half hidden, an interruption in the green
landscape,
Facebook lifts its sculpted roof, metallic, armored, inimical.

But here, in our seclusion, it's all green bushes and bird songs.

We open our books, our journals, preparing to be
enlightened, or at least,
to unburden our minds, gently, and read.

We watch as a bird lands on a high, bushy twig. Nearby.
Wood thrush? Junco?

He settles, shrugs his wings, smooths his gray-and-white
feathers, erupts in
a cascade of complicated song—theme and variations. Then
he's off.

Warbler? Gray Vireo? Not sure, and not wishing to disturb
this idyll,
we take his photograph, slyly, through the windshield. Click.

Soon, our bird, and the renewed trill of song, then, he's off
again,
air-lifting into the high blue.

And repeat, for hours, as his birdly repetitions embroider our afternoon.

Also, twice, from their thicketed nest, a couple of thimble-sized, rust-tinted birds
flit in and out. Swamp sparrows? They do not say.

All afternoon we nestle ourselves in this enchanted tranquility.

Evensong

Like needles of sound,
evening notes rise
from a blackbird's beak.
Behind the row of
trees, their sharp shapes
inked in twilight,
their blacks deep with
the knowledge of light
leaving, of light gone.

As the full moon
burnishes a cloud
floating up there like
a child's bubble, I lie
in my dark, warm bed,
grateful, knowing
myself to be well-loved,
and having settled
myself, am finally
sleeping.

Lyric

The stillness of last night's dew, falling,
The ripeness of the perfect peach,
The coupled sound of two loons, calling,
Two friends' connection, each to each.

The thorny rose's sharp perfection,
Forgiveness offered to a foe,
The firmness of a friend's connection
Though seasons come and seasons go.

A violent thunderstorm retreating,
A candle's flame, however brief,
The sudden joy of kindred meeting,
Or autumn's colors, leaf by leaf.

The promise of a friend's arrival
To plan a meal and dream a dream,
And work together for revival
Of some beloved, forgotten scheme.

Life's rhythmic pulse forever thrumming
in tune with love's eternal song.
Forgive me, if you hear me humming
for joy that you and I belong.

Raven

for Robin

Behold the raven, emissary of inky elegance,
bright of eye, impertinent of aspect, strutting
along our sidewalk this morning on our way to church.

You, Raven, were Noah's emissary after the Deluge,
finding dry ground for survivors marooned in the Ark.
You to whose plumage Solomon's dark hair was

later likened. You and your cohorts daily gathered
morsels of meat and bread to feed Elijah, during Israel's
seven years of starvation and divine retribution.

This very morning we admired your silken plumage,
dark as the burned palm fronds from last Easter's
bonfire, a holy charcoal saved by the priests to mark

our foreheads "penitent" in Lent. Now, Raven, tell us:
Are you Explorer or Trickster? Heaven's messenger
or Devil's spawn? Unashamed thief of shine—

jewels, foil, bright coins, glass, any glitter
for your high, ragged nest—yet also faithful, a spouse
who takes a mate for life, calling me to fidelity.

Last week I found, loose on the ground, a dark
wing feather, a sign I claimed for my desk
(apt plume for poems).

And Raven, it is you who today lent me your name
for my raw, impatient hunger, when I admitted
before the evening meal, "Yes, I am ravenous."

Renegade Otter Terrorizes Surfer

Bellingham Herald, 14 July 2023

You, small, "lovable," slick-furred denizen
of waves and waters, what led you, yesterday,
to terrorize someone surfing your coastal
habitat? You who ride the waves, reclining
indolently on your back as you crack the shells
of clams, cockles, mussels with skill and
exuberance—why not practice common courtesy?
Was it outrage at being seen as "very cute"?
Or, were you simply hungry, chewing away
at that surfer's wooden board as he rode the breakers
you'd always thought of as your personal surf?
What's next, a hostile showdown with sea lions
or an intrusive tugboat? Just settle down, baby.
Be thankful for all that local kelp on the rocks,
so available, so nourishing, and so delicious.

Out Driving, and Its Rewards

(For John Hoyte, on his 91st birthday, with apologies to Billy Collins)

Four p.m. and we'd just returned from a drive,
one of our finest. It was not the easy drive up to the
border (we didn't have our passports with us,
anyway). Nor a drive to the airport (no need to get
out of town). Nor was it the drive to Boulevard Park
to view the sailboats on the bay, where we might have
had to circle fruitlessly for a parking space. Nor
was it the easy drive to Joe's Gardens to choose
plants for my pots on the deck. (Too late for pansies
anyway.) It wasn't along Chuckanut Drive, down
which John always loves to drive slow, admiring
the views, swerving expertly around brutal, ancient
rocks, and under the overarching trees, with glimpses
of Bellingham Bay, and below us, a boat at anchor,
and oyster beds gleaming, polished in the sun.
It was not that drive, with several impatient drivers
behind us, speeding to get somewhere else, and
gracious John pulling over to let them get by. Nor
was it the scenic road up Mt. Baker Highway to the
Douglas Fir Campground, or splendid, foaming
Nooksack Falls, or Heather Meadows, or Artist Point.
No, it was just the five-minute drive to Haggen's

because we were out of butter (we are so often
out of butter), and when we got there someone had
just pulled out from a Handicap Space so we parked
there with our blue-and-white Handicap Placard,
and bought the butter, also John's favorite Gjeltost
Cheese, and a delicious melon that we sliced
open as soon as we got home, and almost at once,
having relieved it of its seeds, we spooned up
its cool, sweet flesh. Yes, it was that drive.

Learning Curve

Thrust into flight by a blue wind, a high cloud
blooms, then seems to halt mid-sky, like a question

asked, waiting for an answer. And look!
There's the silver sliver of the new moon

marked with chalk on heaven's notice board,
announcing a beginning month. We wait, watch,

hoping to write an apt response with words
drawn from the chill on the cheek.

Today the sky is the color I've always imagined
for heaven, a pale cerulean. Young children

seem to know, perhaps informed by memories
of before. Will they teach us? Will we listen?

Now the next cloud is blossoming,
halting mid-sky, then vanishing, an eyelid

closing. Clouds are like that, offering
graphic weather clues, then snatching them back.

In this moment, before winter sets in,
watch with me: what does heaven want

to teach of beauty and impermanence?
Can we take it to heart before it vanishes?

Little Miracle at Shoreline Park

Following an unfamiliar byway in the Bay Area's
drifting fog, I find you,

you, with your almost feral loveliness—a row of trees
anchored in the median on thick, dark trunks,

branches foaming with pale cream blooms
bountiful and downy as fleeces on a flock of sheep.

I leave the car, mosey up close, steal
your likeness, boldly, with my camera's click

and click. Is it unseemly to fall in love with a tree?
Incandescent, ensorceled,

I seize you for memory. I cannot dig you up, cannot
take you home and plant you. I am dismayed

at leaving, not seeing you again. Compulsively
I claim your image to show you to friends.

Back home, I call Eric, who knows things,
and, bless him, he recognizes you, spells you out for me

Melaleuca Alternifolias. Honey Locust, Ti Tree.
I'm holding you here, take a look!

Coda or End-of-Summer Blues

You'd think the season itself would be exhausted,
that we'd be unwilling to pull it all together again
for picnics, tent-camping and opportunities for energetic
night swims, naked, in Bellingham Bay, even awed
as we were at the bio-luminescence that lighted up around us
as we dove in, or stroked out, energetic, across the water.

Here we are, mid-August, 95 degrees, barely a breeze,
barely a bird, all of us drowsing, energy depleted, ready
to give up kitchen duty for a good book, or an
afternoon on the lawn chair with a glass of lemonade.

Regrets: Though the squash blossomed a deep yellow,
it failed to fruit. The rhubarb never achieved its thick
profound pink, and the tomato vines were flecked with
aphids. Even the apple trees, sprayed in spring against
blight, manifested a puny, sour fruit. And my commitment
to pray consistently was inconsistent.

And benefits? Time continues its vigorous life flow,
its force. Spousal love flourishes. Friends visit. Children
thrive. Political news continues to irritate. The seasons pass

with only minor variations. Maybe God is there, awaiting
our attention, loving us, forgiving our careless distraction.

So, what of the season will we remember? What
did we learn that will make next year's season prosper?
Render our own minor contributions more significant?

Yes, Fall will introduce its own challenges
and, perhaps, a smattering of rewards.

Aftermath

Noon, and very quiet. Listen now—
you may hear a murmur under all the other
faint sounds—a hushing in the trees, subdued,
as if branches are still gossiping about
yesterday's storm, lamenting the demise of
half a dozen shattered limbs.

The forest has most of the quiet day
to breathe the green air, to orchestrate birdsong
in the cusp of the tranquil hours, to cradle
half a dozen nests in a geography of twigs.

Afternoon, and with sighs of regret, the forest
accepts the breeze's whispered apology
for breakage. The air clears, admitting
evening light, a radiance low to the ground,
glancing on the roots of grasses, sighting along
the secret vines, and the moss that clothes
rotting logs with an emerald velvet. It is light
that tempers the slow rot of fungi, celebrates
the juice of the ferny succulents tucked away
in the deep heart of the forest.

Autumnal

October, 2023

Now in the days of deepening shadow, time
for the sun, our ancient, constant friend, to travel
south leaving us to shiver, seek, and remember
radiance from the past. As in all seasons, now's
a time for us to practice mercy, to shift from
the unseemly irritation of old angers, renewing
consolation among neighbors and friends, all of us
older than yesterday, me perhaps ambling around
my neck of the woods wearing my comfortably old,
scuffed shoes, passing the time in amicable joke-
and-story-telling. Time to discover whether your
old jeans still fit your even older body, pondering
whether that is a parable of something. Time to lift
an old song into the air, knowing you're missing
some of the words and the high notes. Time to risk
reconnecting with someone you thought you could
never trust again. To listen again to a few bars
of sinewy, difficult orchestral music, hoping that
familiarity will lend it comprehension, or appreciation.
Time to compose a fresh tune to an old ballad (or use
the old tune to carry the original words that just now
re-composed themselves, without effort, in your
inventive mind). Time, now, to search again for

the resolution of lifelong philosophical questions
still unanswered, hanging there, waiting for you in
the realm of mystery. Time to resume that months-ago
hopeful dialog with a friend of the family that got
interrupted. Time to release the emotional hindrances
that still riddle you, stuck in your emotional broom-
closet under the stairs, followed by a prudent decision
to "give it to the universe." Or not. Also, the freedom
within old age's boredom and fatigue to lie down for
a mid-afternoon nap, enjoying the warm drowse of
late Fall, and later, the cool waking again, to the
surprise of sunlight through the open window, you
breathing the pale green breeze, hearing the music of
some early-evening bird. Living with the promise of
returning light that is a heaven-gift. Now, let us all
be glad, not even, always, knowing why, caught
as we are, within some wrinkle in the drift of time.

Berceuse

Though all our blooms have died, though
all the butterflies have butter-flown away,
the garden is not empty. Though along 12th street,
the trees have dropped their leaves, the grass
has withered, weeds flourish unchallenged,
and the blackberries, fruiting weeks ago,
dark-juiced and full of seed, proffer, now,
some of nature's sharpest thorns.

Though in the garden growth is halted,
green thrives, invisible. Beneath the soil,
the beaks of the tulip bulbs, blunted, rest,
hunkered down for a season's long slumber,
like obedient children tucked in to bed. Even
today, though sunlight hours shrink, minute
by minute, now is the season of our gratitude,
as we relinquish our gardens into rest,

But not to die. Expectant life will sleep on,
night by dark night, beneath the snow's
down comforter and the replenishment of roots.
All of it paused for the return of light, of sight,
when the erotic pulse of waking, the throb of
rebirth will arrow up, past old snowdrifts
and the necessity of boots to where in sunlight
waits the deep, free enjoyment of living.

Shift

All night, the stars shift and rearrange,
as if each is saying, "OK, my turn, now,
to be bright and twinkly. You over there,
take time off." My energy is limited.
I watch through the bedroom skylight.
To keep track of the heavenly dance,
I check, and rest, watch, and doze until
morning light fades the sky and finally
sends both me, and the stars, to sleep.

Hidden

How, in winter,
the low light rises
like a bud from its bulb.

Consider, what other treasure
darkness hides, sealed—gold,
crystals, gems deep in rocks
underground!

Un-mined, as yet un-found,
Invisible, even their promise
is uncertain.

Yet, Isaiah tells us, they wait
to be revealed splendid,
jeweled, to the patient,
to the faithful
of heart.

Testaments

Seed

My hope is to secrete within a poem
some minor nugget of gold, or
a scald of steam that generates life,
and if not life, then significant death,
to seed that poem with meanings
subtle enough that they congeal and
become impeccable, like diamonds that
will not dissolve, even in an acid bath.

Do This For Me

My muse, waiting in the wings,
Do this. In the startle of a sudden midnight
let me catch and hold an invitation that is

more than a dream. Though in that dark hour,
I clutch the edge of my sheet in fear of
turning away, let me recognize, in a primitive

skein of language, the fresh gather of
muscular words. Let the gift grip me, then,
in a fine, tenebrous grasp. Like a fabric

of fine silk, let me fold it, fondling it gently
with the fingers of my mind, harnessing
the flow of its lyrical torrent, then,

then spilling its river onto your page.
There now. Let it rest.

The Sound of Rue

That word that names
the mournful awareness of regret,
sounds like complaint, swarms
my writing like bees, like
the groan in my head at today's
fresh onset of words.

Nasturtiums

Here, write it down before it escapes,
flying down the aisle of forgetfulness.
Because you couldn't find your good pen
or your journal, not even the back of
a bill, now the image is gone, gone,
sucked into the bog of unfulfilled verses,
your best phrases that resist remembering.

Was there value in them, anyway? Like
an experimental soup of ingredients,
or summer fruits that never jelled into jam
but ended up as a fresh fruit drink
loved by your convivial friends, gathered,
partying on your deck at sunset.

Just as the sun split at the horizon,
half gone, with the threat of rain by midnight,
you realize you've spent the day taking
the fine weather for granted, not savoring
the brilliant light through the nasturtiums,
their blossoms flaming, there on the deck,
yellow and orange petals fervent enough
to set the house on fire, as if a visiting
angel anointed us with his torch.

You choose words like matches,
striking them to see what happens next.

What Just Happened

"Writing poems moves us past where we were
when we sat down to write them."
—Sharon Olds

How often we find ourselves shoved around
by an interior force, or enchanted by a spell of
ideas in a language we have never mastered
and can barely remember studying. Someone's
sermon, a new novel, even a fresh poem of
one's own, has arrived, uninvited—a visitor
requesting membership in the family.

Phrases suffused with a bright spirit pour into
our minds from someone's far-fingered keyboard,
and then onto a screen. Or a story voiced from
a lectern charges the air with a new energy.
Some refreshing spring we've thirsted for, in
the universal language of love, has taken hold
in us, urging us into deeper listening and thinking.
Some wisdom, sifted, shaped, spoken through
the air, is offered for all of us, its needy inhabitants.

Now, take, eat, drink.

Settling

A writer lifts her head to the sounds of
a recorded voice reading poetry: The words
brush against her ears, seeking a mind
to settle in, with suggestions for the writer herself.
She makes notes in her journal, nailing down
a fresh image or two, setting them down
on the page for further investigation.

She notices how in the evening, the light
filters between the trees, fluidly, finding its way
down to the ground, the way water
flows from the tap between her fingers,
and settles, pooling where it falls.

She smiles, enjoying the intimate comfort
of her cat that has settled in her lap as she writes.
His loud purr assures her: "Thank you for
being warm, and kind, and for the new poems
you are writing while you scratch behind my ears.
Now, do it again. Again. Keep writing.
Settle on a new metaphor. Just don't stop."

The Bright Word

Some words, some narratives
like birds with bright wing feathers, swoop
into the mind, provocative, daring.

Just now, and I mean, two minutes ago,
and *just like that!* a plume arrowed into my head,
from the daily paper.

A mental tingle, a wing of narrative,
flickered, urgent enough to stir my fingers
into word work,

Then, gone. Simply not there—Vanished,
that flaming word—that feather never netted,
barely noted.

Kaleidoscopic, the feathers flashed briefly
in a wideness of air, exiting with barely a shimmer,
blown away, wind-lost.

The Life of I

My “I” seems simple, a stalwart pillar
of the self. So upright a capital, with serifs
above and below for balance, architectural
as a Roman column on its plinth.

By contrast, the lower-case junior “i,”
his tiny bobble-head hovering, waits, devoid
of hope for promotion to a sentence’s start
(though often feeling safe enough at heart).

“I” as capital is a naked leg bone, integer,
personal pronoun and foundational brace, vertical,
righteous, masterful, independent, while hewing
to the line. But if, within a sentence, “I”’s footing

shifts or is, within some strange syntax, rearranged,
see him vulnerable, out of place, a littoral hourglass,
with particles falling, one by one, around his
strict torso, marking his beginning and his end.

The New Poem

You've worked at it for days, this new one, getting it
onto a clean journal page, your pen leaping along,
enthused by the fresh phrases that keep rising
to be recognized. You hesitate briefly, often, listening
for an example that will bring the thing to life,
breathing briefly at a semi-colon, halting at a period.

It needs time to pause, take a break. You let it go,
hoping it will settle. Days later, you're back, ready for
the next stage, the editing. You read it aloud,
eliminating unfortunate phrases, awkward as
mismatched shoes. To bring it to life, you experiment—
trying different line endings and rhyme words.
You smooth stuttering rhythms that jiggle in the poem
like loose change in the pocket. When it steadies,
reading itself back to you with confidence, coherently,
aloud, you let it come to an intelligent end with a sigh
of relief. You blow it a fond, farewell kiss.

The Joy of X

When writing, note how skillfully the symbol X
deletes or changes words, yet cunningly detects
an emotion hidden within the letter's texts.
An act of loving, deeper than mere simple sex,
may quench revenge. And arms, upraised in a simple X
between antagonists, effectively deflects
a violent response. In a stage play, a plot, complex,
may make a forgettable show, but faked sex,
staged for the performance, may be the pretext
for a more dramatic act, making you speculate,
"What's next?"

Freshet

The notes, scribbled untidily, crisp words
leaping from pen to page like adding a sugar
to your morning coffee, then breathless from
activity, the image coming into focus, and a halt,

my pen's aroused, turgid with images, gaining
energy, pausing for a moment at the river's brink
then leaping across from comma to comma, stone
to stepping stone, collecting the body as it quivers,
anticipates the wider reach of a paragraph and finally,
when the metaphor runs out of juice, stopping
at a period, like arriving on the opposite riverbank,
and collapsing, winded, but with sigh
of relief and an Amen like a farewell kiss.

Meal Prep

A fresh poem is, just now, starting to bubble
in my head. I'm chopping vegetables for
a dinner salad, but getting new crisp and juicy
words onto paper seems essential, more
necessary than planning and preparing a meal.

I abandon the salad, focus on a cheese souffle,
a favorite of ours for Sunday dinner. So, into
a resolute fluff of frothy egg whites, I grate
a zesty cheddar, and breaking three eggs and
three yokes to the mix, whip the egg whites
into a favorite of ours, delicious,
and so easy to fix. Coffee ice cream for dessert.

Abandoning the meal, for my friends
I jot on a scrap of paper crunchy words, clues,
possibilities, images like recipes. On my
journal page I mix ingredients—meaty nouns,
salty verbs, a deliciously aged cheddar,
(I know how the cheese bubbles and melts
into a sauce that makes a dish so much better)

a piquant adjective or two—I see them,
hear their syllables in my head, and know

how delicious they will taste. Until, after
a semicolon, the words pause for breath.
And the metaphor, though browning crisply
in the brainpan, is running out of space.
Upon which the poem bursts its bubble,
leaving only a minor dampness on the page.

Returning to the dinner prep, I steam broccoli,
fry the fish, mash the potatoes with sour cream,
still tasting the poem's savory words, still
relishing them like a secret sauce.

How It Happens

When poems begin to arrive they show up
without warning. Yesterday they arrived
late morning, bringing with them bunches of
exotic impressions and nouns with sounds
like bells ringing. For snacks, they unpacked
fragrant adjectives to be nibbled under
the jacaranda trees. I inhaled the syllables' soft
breath, allowing them space to simmer into
wholeness, to find some crisp internal identity,
some fresh, surprising sound or color.
The verbs tend to arrive visibly, like dandelion seeds
that speak themselves into the air. . . . Then,
surprise! a fresh phrase showed up, arriving
tingling, excited to be invited, welcomed to
the party. It's then I begin to sense the phrases
link together and begin thinking back at me,
thinking me in an internal colloquy of response—
interested in how their stanzas sound when
spoken together into the bright air.

This is one of the ways creation happens,
my mind disputing amicably with itself until
freshness breaks in. How a new, crunchy
poem can arrive, impatient, demanding to be
written down. And that is how a poem happens.

Edible Words

If I must eat my words,
or open my mouth to speak
small poems for you

to read at lunch, may they taste
delicious, as nourishing as
manuka honey, that antipodean

sweetness said to heal and
comfort the soul, mend wounds
and correct minor disorders

of the body. After a honeyed
meal, I resolve to speak only truth,
my words rinsing away

falsehood and injury. May my voice
carry mercy music, sweet-tasting,
tingling with a fervent truth.

Sacraments

Guest Room

God, the small room of my heart is getting
so filled with dust and old, odd furniture that
I hesitate to offer you hospitality. Will you look in,
and maybe give me a hand with cleaning up?
Or even, and I know this is a bold and radical idea,
would you move in and live here with me?
It would make me so happy, and feel just right!
You might suggest rearranging the furniture to make it
more welcoming. The window glass is cobwebby,
and when anyone walks in, the floorboards (this is
an ancient house) squeak under the faded rug.
Before you've settled in we could paint the walls
together or, (actually, a fine idea!) hang fresh
wallpaper with a floral pattern in green and gold.
We'd carpet the whole room in some pleasing,
lively shade that I'll leave to your discretion. So,
come in, hang up your coat, unpack, make yourself
at home. Honestly! I'm leaving the door ajar.

Instruction

"The shadow is a necessary teacher."
—Richard Rohr

We cannot truly welcome light until we've
lived a darkness deeper than what nightly
covers the land with its dusky blanket.

After a day vibrating with useful work,
our energies need re-invigoration.
Relinquishment, also, the letting go,

the drift, the abandonment of pride in
accomplishment. For us to hear anything truly,
we must mute the world's noise,

allowing small conversations in the flow
of soul friendship, alone in the hush of
a world asleep, with the quiet night

our essential instructor. In the echo chamber
of the heart, heaven's messages will reach us,
clear as bells.

Re-tuned sensitive as wind instruments,
then, with undivided hearts, we may welcome
good news as it arrives, carried on

pure currents of breath from the mouth of God.

Ladder

For JBNS

Last night I dreamed that
Jacob and I left
the pillow stone
behind us, on the ground.

The ladder was loose
at the bottom.
Unsteady,
under me.

Together, we followed
the dream angels up, up,
rung by golden rung,
climbing that ladder
to heaven, until
we were all out of sight.

The air in the dream
was rare, and soft.

And then, Jacob—
the angels took him,
had him by the hair

and shoulders,
eased his weight
on the ladder.

And then, a strange
thing, he evaporated
into thin air,

and there I was
on the top rung,
alone, afraid to look up
or go back down.

It was a fine view,
but so cold.

Johnny, I thought of inviting you
to join me up there,
but you were chasing
your own dream.

Like Jacob,
you had a journey,
and were on your way
to a foreign land.

Icon

Praying an icon, image edged in gold,
I yearn to enter burning heart of
divine love, the ineffable almost visible.

In this holy flame, kindled, shriven,
my lips touch the edge of a cup of rainwater
like a clue, a breath, until the intimate,
a recognition of the Holy One, arrives.

God's Ear

Tangled, urgent, sprayed from the lips,
the throat, the cries of need travel in tassels—
spider silk, webby, tangled, perhaps ornamented
with a golden pollen of relief or thanks—all of it
entering God's ingeniously shaped ear. Need
and gratitude mingled, emergent, seething like
sweet smoke, and then what? How? Woven with
a carpet of others, how are the prayers dissected,
separated, reedy fibers traced back to each wide pain,
each cry smelling of its unique smoke of anguish?
Even minor songs, troubled, may release a fragrance
pungent as spice in God's nostrils. Wait, confident
it will matter, without further investigation.

Invitation

In the mouth of a truth-teller, speaking
with the integrity of love, every word, painful
or profound, turns hallowed. How, then, to find
the courage to speak with such authenticity,
with words muscular enough to ring the doorbell
of the listener's mind, admitting the rigor and
the glory of the holy through the open door of
the down-to-earth, the commonplace, the very
ordinary.

Now, un-self us from our casual
selfishness. Forgive our un-forgiving-ness.
Loose from us those cursory confessions, half
truths spoken with spurious intention—to
release us, shallowly, from guilt, to make us feel
less culpable, more holy. As we meet and enter
the dining room of truth and grace, let us join
and feed together on holy food, prepared and
provided by our welcoming Host.

Queries in Time of Plague

We call on you, Creator. Adjust
our souls, our human psyches, to the
vagrant reality of living in this tempestuous
century. Ravaged by anxiety, torn apart
by possibility of sudden death, we live in
fear of infection, of the power of an
interloper, too small to see, that escapes
our vision, slipping past our most cunning
face masks. We yield ourselves to the ministry
of physicians and their medications, of
sharp needles-full of inactivated viruses.
We swallow capsules of prevention.
Night by night we wake, the body-soul
continuum within us crying for a renewal
of health. Troubled, nightly, with a sinus ache
and a dry cough, fear for our fruitful lives
is magnified in an un-answering darkness.
We shoot our arrows of need into a void,
hoping that we are vindicated in our
struggles, in our hope of staying alive.

How to justify our existence? Fragments,
we hurtle, alone in the expanding, out-
rushing universe of cold stars, wayward comets.
Of black holes that suck in their own reality.

Why? How? When, may we, in our fragile
humanity, persist and even flourish?

Plaint

I want spiritual vigor enough for
an hour of effort, with energy
to open a window, inhale the wide air,
pray my complaint. Yet I face
the scourge of uncertainty.

As I polish silver, peel potatoes,
brave fatigue, rebuke pain, trample
weeds of distraction, I mow down
the tedious turf of dailiness,
tread disappointment's sharp,
gray gravel underfoot.

Until finally, I shift that
untidy parcel, and fasten it
to the shoulder of God,
my fellow traveler.

Prayer in Lent

Save me from cursory confession, from
half-truths voiced without conviction,
admissions spoken with spurious ease, the words
sliding off my tongue with little forethought,
lightly, as if simple speaking renders me
more holy, less moved by guilt.
So, now, the list: forgive my unforgiving-ness,
the cravings of my life for recognition, not
for you. Un-self me of my routine selfishness.
Strip off the borrowed finery, the routine
complacency of my faith, and may my nakedness
prove to be my utmost truth.

Lucky

Lucky simply means blessed, a state
of being we reach not through labor, but
by embrace of this very day in Creation,
this God-blessed day with its early
radiance breaking, a signal freshly sent
from You, our world's true Light.

Yesterday's threatening clouds,
with messages of peril and uncertainty,
remind us that it's in shadow we may
learn the blessing of waiting, watching
for the out-breaking of light. Let us lift
hands and hearts to You. Free us from
doubt and impulses that divert our souls
from your bright holiness.

May You, our living God, who delights
in our delight, ignite in us fresh visions
of Yourself and your transfixing love.

Questions Like Ants

Like ants, the questions nag and press, sometimes
single file, but too often in a small army that
blocks my lines of sight to Heaven. Sometimes
visible enough for me to cut them off at the pass,
but mostly closer, too close, the straggling clots of
black bodies nip and pinch at my soul skin,
trying to carry away any crumbs of elliptical faith
in an interior out of sight of everyone but me.

Because I know. Because I feel their itch and jostle,
the soul irritants. Because I'm crying out, "O God.
God, what am I to do? How do I find a way
to the other side?" Often uncertainties un-faith me,
snipping at my garment of salvation, leaving me
naked, clutching at words in the accusatory air,
as I hold around me, shivering, mere shreds of
salvific belief in you, the only deity I know about.
I've argued with You for years, have waited, silent,
unwilling, unable to give up. Come, now. Fill
the gaps, mend the widening cracks in my aging
soul. I move more slowly now, see more dimly,
require more daily. But I'm moving in your direction.

Storm/Calm

"The sea lay down, silky and sorry"
—Mary Oliver

Mary Oliver's poem
rises off the page
to retell the story—Galilee,
and the lake roiled by
that unruly wind,
and the men in the boat
panicking, and calm
Jesus with them.

Their faces show
what terror looks like.
Until. Until two kinds
of power collide. And
when weather gives in
(each ripple an apology),
fright drains from the men's
faces and their bones,
replaced by awe, as the One
among them shows both
weather and those human
beings, what saving
power looks like.

It is then that purpose
begins its growth among them,
and a new knowing,
and power for miracle
almost as great as the event
enacted on Galilee.

The Art of Alteration

Alter, and *anew*, two words within the trope
of doubled syllables, also, a twofold clue
to the possible, for fresh chances to review
mere wishful thinking, or the vitalizing hope
of leaving the old behind, and moving into
something brisk and bracing, something new.

Also, more opportunities for future growing,
replete with variations for all those dearly
needed changes that form our inventive knowing
and a more fertile maturity, clearly
not yet within our reach. But, nearly!

The Eagles

Above our heads the raptors wheel and float. And we
observe, with what elemental artistry,

their flying shadows move across the grass,
patterning the earth beneath them as they over-pass.

Their fluid ease of movement through the air
seems like a kind of miracle. And anywhere

an eagle flies, she journeys to discover
fresh mountains, shores and seas to hover over.

Perhaps our souls' approach to God is, "always pray,
but learn from eagles' flight, watching the way

they fling their feathered bodies through the sky,
trusting in heaven's mercy as they fly."

Mortality

Tell me, how may I delay my dying? I throb,
drowning in language. The desire to live on
in words has stirred me since very young.
How can I reverse this human entropy?

I, who felt an *élan vital* navigating
a dozen unspoiled paradises, photographing
the sequenced beauties of forest or field,
struggle now to rise from a chair. My eyes fight
to read a map. Dreaming the alien radiance
of fireflies, I wake, buckled to earth, shadowed by
a mortal gravity. I breathe deeply, loving
the taste of air, the scents of flowered fields,
constrained also to examine the grit
of sour gravels, the rot of leaves.

How carelessly, lightly, often I used to laugh!
Now, with sunlight dancing on the feathered
heads of grasses under my fingers, I know as well
their destiny—to die under winter's chill, or with
the dearth of rain. Longing for an easy departure,
I dread the prospect of decline. Tell me, where
may I find consolation for mortality? How escape
that deep gash, the inevitable wound of death?
Where may I find a final healing, an infinite health?

Breath

As a child I used to think if I
held my breath I could stop time. As
a child so much is possible. . . .

Today, in another state, a friend
of my heart is dying. Is almost dead.
Throat paralyzed, I'm dumb
to frame words of comfort, to call on
divine power to bring relief.

My lack of language feels physical,
like losing an arm. Will it help
if I pray, in silence, pressing out
the words from within my own need?

I grasp for a prayer sinewy enough
to bring comfort to his body
once throbbing with health. And
for my troubled heart, my common,
lovely life, allow fresh strength.

Mouth to Mouth

You showed up, a food basket
on Your right arm, and to drink,
a full thermos of lemonade. There,
under a shade tree, a linden, You spoke.

Your words—I inhaled them, drinking
deep from Your gallon mouth,

Until all the old pain became for me a kind of
holy food, and the tears flowed, a fresh
river, water for cleansing, for ongoing life.

Acknowledgments

The Christian Century—

"Settling," "Queries," "Leaving," "The Bright Word,"

"Mosquito Lake Road"

Whale Road Review—

"Bleed"

Calf—

"Bleed"

"Afternoon River"

About Paraclete Press

Paraclete Press is the publishing arm of the Cape Cod Benedictine community, the Community of Jesus. Presenting a full expression of Christian belief and practice, we reflect the ecumenical charism of the Community and its dedication to sacred music, the fine arts, and the written word.

SCAN TO READ MORE

www.paracletepress.com

O that my words were written down!
O that they were inscribed in a book!
O that with an iron pen and with lead
they were engraved on a rock forever!

—Job 19:23–24

Outcast and utterly alone, Job pours out his anguish to his Maker. From the depths of his pain, he reveals a trust in God's goodness that is stronger than his despair, giving humanity some of the most beautiful and poetic verses of all time. Paraclete's Iron Pen imprint is inspired by this spirit of unvarnished honesty and tenacious hope.

You may also be interested in...